My Lovely Golden Rose

A Lifetime of Poetic Reflections and Precious Memories

Carrolyn Pichet

AuthorHouse™
1663 Liberty Drive
Bloomington, IN 47403
www.authorhouse.com
Phone: 1-800-839-8640

Front Cover Design by Céline Pichet

Published by AuthorHouse 01/20/2014

ISBN: 978-1-4918-4865-4 (sc)
ISBN: 978-1-4918-4864-7 (hc)
ISBN: 978-1-4918-4862-3 (e)

Library of Congress Control Number: 2013923785

This book is printed on acid-free paper.

Contents

Belief in God

Love and Romance

Guest Poets -- All in the Family

Potpourri

My Legacy in Poetry and Prose

Dedication

To My Beloved Sister, Gloria,
With Eternal Gratitude for your
wonderful influence on my life,
Every thought of you brings renewed strength and love,
You will always be in my heart and
a big part of who I am, and
I'm truly grateful the for the nurturing you gave me,
For providing me with the positive
perspective that only a sister could.
Thank you for being there for me when I needed you most.

Love always,
Carrolyn

Perspectives

Sometimes in life we meet a person who is able to look deep into our souls and uncover that intimate secret within. And sometimes we find a person who possesses the ability to express that intimacy in warm, soothing terms. But rarely do we find a person owning both talents as we do in the author, Carrolyn Pichet.

Ms. Pichet grasps seemingly ordinary people, events and ideas in our lives and paints them in warm and gentle terms that rekindle memories and satisfy our wish to encapsulate them in our hearts and minds forever. Readers will realize a familiarity with the author's characters and relate them to their own lives. Ms. Pichet also recognizes poetic potential in others and she has included, along with her own poetry, several unpublished works she has gathered.

---- ***Shirley L. Marshall, sister***

With adventure of mind and the soul of a poet, Carrolyn Pichet has published two books, *The Best Is Yet to Come* and *Growing Up in the Nation's Capital.* An avid lover of words with the gift of using them with artistic beauty, she enjoys interpreting poetry, telling stories and creating beautiful images. *My Lovely Golden Rose* is her first book of poetry. After you savor this treasure, share it with your friends and family. They will thank you for it.

---- ***Edna L. Bowie, aunt***

My Lovely Golden Rose is a gift of love from Carrolyn Pichet to her family and friends. She has gathered a bouquet of poems from her treasure trove of writings and has also included a section for the contributions of her family.

This is her first book of poetry and hopefully it will not be her last. In her two books of prose, *The Best Is Yet to Come* and *Growing Up in the Nation's Capital,* we discovered her subtle wit and keen sense of humor. However, her true gift is found in her poetry.

With simple elegance, she introduces unforgettable characters who remind us of our better selves. Her verses reach into our hearts and elicit emotions long buried. Vivid images transport the reader to a place of beauty and wonder.

I invite you to experience the love Carrolyn offers in this little jewel. Her poetry speaks compellingly of her love for her God, her family and her country.

---- ***Marilyn Bowie-Coates, cousin***

From the Author

My how time flies. It seems like only yesterday that I started writing poetry. And yet, it was 25 years ago when I realized that my life would never be the same. After the sudden loss of my beloved sister Gloria, I became more sensitive to my surroundings -- to people, to nature, to life -- to everything. I became closer to God because I needed a friend who would always be there for me. Since that time everything has had new meaning for me. I am profoundly touched by the beauty I find everywhere. I am deeply moved by the wonderful things created by His hands.

Years have passed and yet my life has remained essentially the same. Over the years my life experiences have been subtly incorporated into my writing, often mirroring the images of my soul. I feel very blessed and hope I can gently lure you into my world with my thoughts, imagery and words. I reflect my Grandmother Helen's legacy throughout this collection with intricately detailed stories, fantasy tales, flashbacks and even bits and pieces of my own life. I want to share some of my special moments with you. We can all learn to smile, laugh, live and love. I invite you to join me now and we'll share these experiences together. As you read, close your eyes and let yourself be lulled into my *Lifetime of Poetic Reflections and Precious Memories.*

Family

To Gloria with Love

On a quiet autumn morning
I saw a white turtledove,
Whose mate, hovering not far away,
Was cooing with tender love.

And as I watched that peaceful scene,
Loving thoughts came to me,
And I felt your gentle presence near,
As you returned to my memory.

You come to me in curious ways,
Like the essence of exotic perfumes,
Extracts from nature's loveliness,
From a garden in full bloom.

Tufts of white cotton in powder blue skies,
Billions of stars twinkling at night,
The call of a whippoorwill to his love,
A hummingbird poised in flight.

A garden of potpourri in springtime,
A mixture of fragrant flowers,
The sweet, spiced aroma of cinnamon,
The clean, fresh air after showers.

Lush green carpet on the forest floor,
A purple-blue ceiling in a storm,
Red velvet drapes of roses grown,
The golden chandelier lighting each morn.

Now and then something special occurs,
And it serves to let me know,
That after each storm comes serenity,
From the reposing colors of a rainbow.

You're always here within my heart,
In the things I see and hear,
I need only to wish it so,
And like magic you appear.

Sometimes you're in the things I feel,
The warmth of sun-bleached sand,
The refreshing coolness of summer rain,
The silky touch of a newborn's hand.

Thoughts of you bring me happiness,
They fill my heart with melodies,
Though each bird's song is unique only to him,
Together they make a harmonious symphony.

I feel your presence every day,
In things that bring me pleasure,
And I carefully wrap each precious thought,
To place in my own life's treasures.

Your love and wisdom guide me still,
For the things I say and do,
Are never mere words or idle deeds,
But touched and inspired by you.

And so I thought you'd like to hear,
That I'll forever keep you close to me.
Dear sister, you are My Lovely Golden Rose
In my book of precious memories.

Who Would Have Thought?

Who would have thought that my tiny girl with brilliant black eyes,
Who demanded much attention with her persistent cries,
Who walked and talked well before it was time,
Would be an enigma personified, this daughter of mine.

Who would have believed that you stuck like "Elmer's" glue,
Shy, apprehensive, often concealing the real you,
Big hearted, playful, mischievous and funny too,
Trying hard to please me in everything you do.

How could I have suspected that in your teenage years,
You'd be living with a phone growing out of your ears.
That you'd lay siege to the bathroom, your favorite place,
Where you'd spend countless hours making up your face,

Where the mirror has become your very best friend,
And dressing up lasts for hours on end.
It never occurred to me how fast you'd grown,
'Til my clothes and perfumes you claimed as your own.

You often fall asleep with one ear to the phone,
And the caretaker of your room must be a cyclone.
Clothes thrown haphazardly in unimaginable places.
Wild clothes, crazy hairstyles, not to mention those braces!

I never could have dreamed that the same little girl
Would be so beautiful today -- a rare cultured pearl.
But if I could choose a precious gem from long ago,
It would have to be the loveliest black cameo.

I sincerely hope that your future will be bright,
That you'll keep moving forward, always doing what's right.
And that you continue to be loving, caring and unselfish too.
And remember my daughter, I'll be there for you.

Listen, My Son

Sit down, I want to have a word with you, my son.
About some of the wild, foolish things you've done.
Listen to your mother's sincere plea.
And strive to be what you were meant to be.

You've made some mistakes, all humans do.
But the time has come to put the past behind you.
You're still young and strong and you have a good heart.
My son, it's time for you to make a fresh start.

Yes, I know this is your life, you can selfishly say,
But there are many people who don't see it that way.
Your wife and children, to mention a few,
And there are others who love you, who care about you.

You don't want your own son to grow up alone,
Without the presence of his daddy at home.
As he grows up in this hard world year after year,
He'll need both his mother and father near.

Growing up without parents is cruel and sad.
Be there for him, make him proud of his dad.
When you hold him, touch him, when you kiss his face.
Give him your love wrapped in your tender embrace.

Later on when your so-called "friends" cross your path,
Look them in the eyes, take a deep breath and have a good laugh!
Tell them you're not into wrongdoing, whatever it may be,
That you've taken charge of your own destiny.

They'll be back, believe me, to lead you astray.
Tell them to keep walking and stay out of your way.
You want no part of it, believe it! Son, I know you can.
For your beautiful family, you must be a man.

To err is human, to forgive divine, as it's often said.
God has forgiven, forgive yourself, and hold high your head.
Make each decision with your loved ones in mind.
And remember, son, it's their future that's on the line.

Memories of My Dad

When I was just a baby girl
And my father held my hand,
I felt a warmth I've never found
With any other man.

To see that smile upon his face,
To look into his eyes,
Would make storm clouds disappear,
Roll back the ocean tides.

The wrinkles that graced his forehead,
From a lifetime of frowns and smiles
Resembled a bird of paradise
Flying him over life's miles.

His gentle ways filled my life
With a love meant just for me
But each one of us felt that way
There were four of us kids, you see.

The many times he held me close,
So handsome, dark and tall,
And helped me through life's little woes,
Never letting me stumble and fall.

My memories over the years reveal
What a wonderful father he was,
The moments we spent together then
Mean even more to me now because,

Of all the loves I'll ever have
He is surely the only man
Who helped fulfill my childhood dreams
And made me who I am.

Remembering with the fondest thoughts
The wonderful times we had
I still find happiness and joy
In the memories of my Dad.

My Mother Is a Gem

Some folks look for treasures,
In rivers, mines and mountain caves,
Others seek out life's pleasures,
Far beneath the ocean waves.

I've found a world of riches,
Without hard work or traveling far,
My mom is a gem, a jewel,
My mother is a star.

She's a jewel of rare beauty,
A diamond in the rough,
Refined, elegant, polished,
Hand faceted, carefully buffed.

She's the light that always guides me,
When at times I go astray,
Leading me gently back to the fold,
Each time I lose my way.

Welcoming me like a prodigal daughter,
Healing hurts, wiping away my tears,
Comforting me when I'm in pain,
Encouraging, nurturing through the years.

A woman first, but always a mother,
Lovely and poised, with such a loving soul,
Making sacrifices for others,
Motivated by a heart of gold.

Working hard to raise four children,
Praising little accomplishments and deeds,
Intelligent, artistic and dignified,
Selflessly tending to our needs.

She's gentle, so very gentle,
When mending broken hearts,
But solid like the rock of ancient temples,
In the discipline she imparts.

Age has now bent her shoulders,
Soft, cotton-white hair crowns her head,
The years have carved wrinkles in her brow,
And a slight stoop marks her tread.

Of course there are "lapses" in memory,
And the aches and pains often appear,
So we look for reasons to tell her,
That she's loved more every year.

Don’t spend your precious hours,
Looking for riches in silver and gold,
While you’re seeking worldly treasures,
Your loved ones are getting old.

Be attentive to those who are near you,
And I know that you’ll come to see,
You can find many precious treasures,
Right there in your own family.

If you wait until it’s too late,
You’ll the regret things you haven’t told,
Say them now, and you’ll add a blessing,
And help ease the pain of growing old.

My mother is a gem,
Sparkling, fine and rare,
She’s loving, lovely, loved,
And we let her know we care.

Sisters

Is it strange to tell you I love you,
And to let you know that I care,
Or to tell you I think I'm lucky,
And glad we have so much to share?
Remember when we were just children?
We were inseparable right from the start,
Born under the same zodiac sign,
Only one year and four days apart.

We always stayed close to each other,
The reason is not hard to explain,
Our personalities are almost molded into one,
Like two candles lit with one flame.
You thought I was your own little baby,
And I always felt that I was,
So I never wanted to change things,
It was fun being "yours" because,

With you I was never afraid or lonely,
You were always by my side,
For me you fought many a battle,
And wiped big, wet tears from my eyes.
In spite of our wild childhood scuffles,
We knew it was meant to be that way,
But if anyone else tried to divide us,
They soon came to rue that day.

How can I call you Big sister,
When you're shorter in stature, it's true,
You make up the difference on the inside,
In strength, wisdom and courage too.
Is it weird what we have together,
A relationship as deep as can be,
I've looked up to you all my life,
And all your life you've been there for me.

So I'll always admire you dear sister,
You're funny, witty and smart,
More than just a friend and confidante,
And I love you with all my heart.
Is it odd that I've confessed my secret,
Or unusual that I want you to know,
That I cherish each moment we're together,
Is that strange? No, I don't think so.

My How You've Grown

My, how you've grown my son
You've become so handsome and tall
Seems like only a year ago
You were asking for your first football.
You made it through the terrible two's
And survived the dangerous teens
You reached the threshold of manhood
Much faster than I ever dreamed.

Many of your friends didn't make it
Some serving time, others are dead
You passed through the maze of peer pressure
And made us proud just like you said.
We've had good times and bad times together
Been over ups and downs, thick and thin
We tackled and healed your growing pains
A new life for you was about to begin.

Don't think it's all over between us
There'll be other times to rally together
But now you'll be able to ride the tides
Return safely to port after stormy weather.
There'll be many issues to confront in life
That will put your courage to the test
Tough decisions to make, many crossroads to take
Somehow, I know you'll do your best.

Obstacles will be put in your pathway
There'll be moments of hardship and pain
But you will make it to the top
Even if you must start all over again.
The time has come to let you go
Dear son, I must set you free
I'll watch you test your wings with pride
But it won't be easy for me.

Hopefully there will come a day
Perhaps when you have a wife and child
You'll look back on the things we shared
And think of them as being worthwhile.
Go, my son and conquer the world
Have a life full of excitement and fun
I'll be sitting back just shaking my head
Saying, "My, how you've grown my son."

Have You Met My Aunt Edna?

Have you met my remarkable Aunt Edna?
Well, here's one thing that you should know,
Make no mistake, she has that unique "Auntie" glow,
She's that very special Aunt, you know the one,
Her smile warms your heart like the morning sun,
One well-chosen word can make tears disappear,
Her comfort blanket of love chases away your fears,
A special hug tells you that you're the most precious of all,
She'll pick you up and brush you off, but she'll never let you fall.

Have you met my amazing Aunt Edna?
She's cute and delicate -- actually she's quite small,
Tipping the scales at 95 pounds, standing a mere 5 feet tall,
But she's endowed with such an enormous heart,
There's a powerhouse of life's lessons in the advice she imparts,
She has weeded her own garden so only the loveliest flowers bloom,
Her humble presence spreads fragrance to every corner of the room,
But don't take her too seriously; she's the ultimate barrel of fun,
A living testament to life's battles she's fought and won.

Have you met my "cool" Aunt Edna?
She's a treasure trove of the quaintest expressions,
Each colorful proverb teaching life's valuable lessons,
And she strategically uses them to let you know,
There are things you shouldn't do, places you dare not go,
She can see through your little lies, hear false notes in your song,
She'll tell you in no uncertain terms if what you're doing's wrong,
Gentle yet persuasive, sensitivity and kindness come first,
Her winning smile and sparkling eyes are both a blessing and a curse.

Have you met my awesome Aunt Edna?
At eighty-nine years old she's still going strong,
With mind and body in perpetual motion all day long,
Still fearlessly driving, line-dancing, enjoying hours of shopping,
With few signs of slowing down and no intention of stopping,
Her plans for the future stretch well beyond ninety-nine,
Sitting around idle would be just wasting her time,
We have to work hard to keep up with her pace,
She's still a bundle of energy, thanks to God's grace.

Have you met my gracious Aunt Edna?
With deep compassion she spreads joy around,
Good will and generosity of spirit make up her crown,
Her wisdom and mediation skills alleviate stress and strife,
She's a big piece of heaven, a slice of the good life,
Going out of her way to help or to give you a hand,
To overcome barriers, convincing you that you can,
Building your confidence, showing that others care.
In times of need she's the very first one there,

Have you met my special Aunt Edna?
She's special in so many ways,
Doing immeasurable deeds that deserve our praise,
She rules with a heart that's patient and kind,
With selflessness and humility foremost in her mind,
She's a rare gift sent to us from heaven above,
Who gives of herself with a heart full of love,
Going through her life with her eyes on the prize,
Beneath her dignified elegance, she's an angel in disguise.

Have you met my fantastic Aunt Edna?
If you've missed her there's something you must do,
Look around for the treasure most valuable to you,
One of life's precious gems--a ruby, or perhaps a pearl,
Seek out the most beautiful person ever to grace your world,
Someone who believes that you're the most precious too,
Giving an abundance of love, she's like a second mother to you,
She's been with you through thick and thin, in good and bad weather,
Then that person you've found is surely YOUR Aunt Edna.

Have you met my precious Aunt Edna?
She's like the most inspiring words or thoughts in your mind,
Like the softest velvet, the smoothest silk, the gentlest breeze of all time,
She's the melodious tunes of songbirds each time they take flight,
And every reflection or silhouette that silently floats into sight,
She's the taste of sweet nectar as a single red rose bursts into bloom,
She's every positive emotion we experience when she walks into a room,
As sure as pastel rainbows transform the heavens after stormy weather,
Proud generations will cherish our Aunt Edna forever.

My Other Lovely Family

You may already know how wonderful it is to have a loving family,
To enjoy love, comfort, pleasure and fun together constantly,
There's support and encouragement for everything you say and do,
I'm twice as lucky when it comes to loving families--I've got more than two.

Let's get on with my amazing story, one that I really love to tell,
My new family appeared from out of the blue, like a magician's spell,
In another country, an unknown village that I visited so many years ago,
I met some of the most wonderful people that in my lifetime I'll ever know.

How it happened is a bit unusual, it's really quite extraordinary,
Perhaps a magic wand, mysterious cloud or pixie dust launched my story,
As the invited guest of a Frenchman on my first trip to a foreign land,
The good folks in that far away place eagerly took me by the hand.

We met on a snowy slope for a day of sleigh riding and fun,
This group of complete strangers made my first visit a happy one,
That was right down my alley, sleighing down on that hill,
They invited me to join them with sincere warmth and good will.

To make a long story short, my life changed that same day,
Later I had to choose to return home or to marry and stay,
I made the right choice, no doubt in my mind, I say this true,
My decision changed the course of my life; it made me a winner too.

There's no better love than those gentle hearts I hold dear,
Than the loving folk who accepted me into their lives that first year,
Now there are nieces and nephews; little ones all around,
And to think that it all started in the new world that I found.

Such genuine, kind souls who took to me that special day,
Welcoming a total stranger and encouraging her to stay,
Over the years many joys among us we've shared, so you see,
I'm grateful for their love; it was certainly meant to be.

You've heard me brag and boast about how good life can be,
That's because I have a beautiful extended French family,
I believe it's more than mere luck; it's most definitely destiny,
That God gave me another lovely family living across the sea.

My heart swells with love when I write since we're often far apart,
I'm still a big part of their lives because I never leave their hearts,
I'll forever cherish this family, and know they feel the same about me,
When my thoughts turn to them, I think with a smile, *C'est la vie.*

Welcome to Our World, Precious Baby Girl

So glad you finally arrived, healthy, well and so fine,
You're beautiful inside and out, of sound body and mind,
While we anxiously waited for your grand entrance,
We knew you'd capture our hearts at first glance.

When you opened your bright eyes that very first day,
Your loving family had worked hard to pave the way,
For you to have peace, serenity, strength and so much love,
They prayed to our Heavenly Father to bless you from above.

We know you'll be successful in whatever you do,
That there are wonderful things in store for you,
And because you're our baby, we'll always love you too.
Because you're a child of God, He'll be there to protect you.

Welcome to Our World, Precious Baby Girl!

Renewing Spirits, Restoring Souls

The Life of the Party (A Tribute to Carl E. Cross)

He was the life of every party, my cousin CC,
He was everything we could want and expect him to be,
He gave the shirt off his back, shared his last dime,
He lifted our spirits with joy, time after time.

Laughing, loving and graciously living every moment, hour and minute,
Doing things with him was such fun because he put all of his heart in it.
His enthusiasm was contagious and so was his winning smile,
He drew everyone to him with his caring, passionate style.

Making others feel welcome, sharing his love all around,
Whenever CC was present endless laughter could be found.
Among family, neighbors or friends, it didn't matter who,
His heart beat with the inner peace each one of us knew.

He beamed light out of darkness, creating memories that will forever last,
And now our Master has called CC home to fulfill an extraordinary task.
Out of all of the heavenly assignments, he'll like nothing more,
Than to lead the Welcoming Committee for new souls through heaven's door.

Carl has been given a wonderful job in God's temple, he must be pleased,
That he was specially chosen to fulfill this heartwarming deed.
The duty is lovingly greeting, talking and hugging at the Pearly Gates,
Inviting all God's children home, helping them to rejoice and celebrate.

And so we are truly grateful and feel more than blessed,
That our Father has called Carl to receive his ultimate happiness,
We thank Him for allowing us to share this precious love.
And we'll have Carl's wonderful welcome when we're called home above.

Where the Angels Fly

Ever wonder what's beyond the crystal blue sky?
Where the sun warms the day,
And the moon lights the way,
It's a place where the Angels fly.

Flowers and trees in a sweet scented breeze,
Where the birds come to nest,
Where children play, laugh and sing all day,
And there's only joy and happiness.

For there's a Good Shepherd waiting there,
To welcome each new face,
To that home above and with words of love,
He bids them to take their place.

"Suffer Little Children, Come Unto Me,"
To God's great kingdom on high,
Where you'll find eternal peace,
Up here, where the Angels fly.

Each time you look beyond the clouds,
That ray that lights the sky,
Is your Angel smiling back at you
From that place where the Angels fly.

Brothers

Brothers are a very special breed,
That no words can quite portray,
The little winks and smiles exchanged,
The thoughts you shared along the way.

Big brothers are often more than that,
A source of strength and pride,
With love and guidance, they show the way,
During talks and long walks side by side.

Little brothers often bring us joy,
And much happiness as well.
The fun, the games and special jokes,
That only brothers understand so well.

The years passed by and then one day,
Your little brother became a man,
But big brother always stayed close by,
To lend him a helping hand.

And because of that special bond you had,
You wish he could be with you still,
But he'll stay right there within you heart,
And you know that he always will.

So many things you wish you'd said,
So many things left undone,
What brothers feel is deeper than words,
Your bond was a special one.

It does not matter how or why
Your brother left so fast
Time spent with him was wonderful,
And that's why memories last.

So cherish those precious moments,
Of the times that together you shared,
And may they bring you comfort now,
Knowing that he knew how much you cared.

A Mother's Love

In my garden some time ago, I planted many seeds.
Some blossomed, others bloomed, and a few turned into weeds.
And in my garden there grew a bush of roses, sweet and fair.
I watered, pruned and cared for it, with a mother's tender care.
Upon my bush there bloomed a rose, so strong and yet so fine,
And through the years it grew to be the only one of its kind.

Then one day it simply fluttered away, to Heaven, I am told.
As the angels kissed that lovely rose, its petals turned to gold.
Though words will never be enough, I hope this poem will do,
To let you know how very much our thoughts are there with you.
And so I chose a single rose to show you that we care,
And that others know the pain you feel, the burden that you bear.

Somehow I know your lovely rose that flew on wings of a dove,
In beauty and spender forever blooms in His garden up above.
Forever cherish your golden rose, as a symbol of a mother's love.
May God in heaven bestow on you, His blessings from above.
May He give you added strength and help to ease your pain,
And may He bless and keep you 'til you hold your rose again.

A Tribute to a Great Lady

We've all been friends for quite some time, it's true,
You led us, comforted us, and yes, cajoled us too,
So very smart, even extraordinary in many ways,
Worthy of admiration, winning our love, earning our praise,

Thinking we knew it all, if some problems we raised,
Your intelligence would bedazzle us, leaving us dazed.
Strong mentor, excellent teacher, a good friend to know,
Quietly taking us under your wing, helping us to grow.

Teaching us to organize a meeting, or how to vote yes or no!
We're grateful now, that you worked hard, cared for us so.
Influencing the big things, little things that we do,
Yes, we shall carry on and when each day is through,

All said and done, in our minds this thought rings true,
In our tribute to a Great Lady, *Une Grande Dame,*
We must give credit and honor where it's due,
You've profoundly touched us, done so much in our lives,
That we'll forever cherish fond memories of you.

What an Awesome God We Serve

We mourn the loss of a good son, brother, father and friend,
Our Father was with him over the miles and across the sea,
He sent an angel to bring him here to his earthly home,
To bid us farewell.

Your son fulfilled all of the duties God entrusted to him on earth,
And we know he performed them well,
A special person, he was chosen to enter into our Father's temple,
Where he will forever abide, realizing an important mission for God.

No need ask how he is; we know that he is wrapped in God's Goodness,
We all know where he is; he is Standing Tall in God's Kingdom,
Where the streets are paved with gold; where lions sleep with lambs,
And the winds are lifted up by fluttering wings of angels.

We know that he has been called by God to his eternal home,
Where there is much work for him, and he will do that well too,
He completed his earthy chores, doing wonderful things,
Now God needs him for a heavenly task, and that has already begun.

In quiet of night a mom saw the angel soar off to fetch her beloved son,
To carry him on wings to that heavenly abode,
Where the Lord had prepared a place for him,
Among the Good Shepherd's flock, basking in God's Glory.

To God we give the glory and we sing praises to the Lord,
We thank Him for his mercy and for sharing this life with us,
Through the grace of God, His amazing grace,
Until you meet him again in that Sacred, Holy Place.

What a Mighty God! What an Awesome God we serve.

The Day He Called You Home

That day was quiet and serene,
Calm, just like you've always been,
There was a hushed echo, an audible silence,
Much like the tranquil aurora of your presence,
The day was as pure as the blanket of fresh-fallen snow,
A blizzard day not seen in more than a century,
Everything was done especially for you that blessed day.
What A Merciful God is He!

When the Master invited you into His waiting room,
He put a shawl around your shoulders. He held your hand,
While His angels prepared your place at His table,
And made everything comfortable, so beautiful.
When their task was done and all was ready to receive you,
He softly called you home in a warm, sweet whisper,
God's call exemplified His love for you.
What A Loving God is He!

Perhaps you heard the rustle of feathers,
The soft fluttering wings of angels,
Coming to take you home,
With gentle arms outstretched to guide you,
To your special place in His kingdom,
To receive your reward for a job well done,
To dwell where love and peace abide.
What A Wonderful God is He!

We feel your presence everyday in our hearts and minds,
Helping to soothe our pain away after you said goodbye,
We'll miss you dearly, but we have wonderful memories,
How thankful we are for the time you spent among us,
Sharing your life for just a little while,
Vibrant, invigorating, your enthusiasm inspiring,
Know that you'll stay forever in our hearts.
What An Awesome God is He!

Listen to the harmonious voices of the angelic choir,
As they celebrate your arrival with a joyful noise unto Him,
We lift our hands towards the heavens in praise,
Singing hallelujah, hallelujah, you are going home!
Hallelujah. Praise His holy name,
That will be such a glorious day when we meet again,
And you know that we will all see you then!
What a Mighty God is He!

St Peter and Bob

As St Peter stood before Heaven's Pearly Gates,
A long line a newcomers patiently waits,
Standing proud and tall, eyes filled with grateful tears,
On the threshold of heaven at the appointed time and date.

St Peter glanced at the list he'd prepared well beforehand,
Then stared at the horizon of that sacred land,
I'm looking for someone I don't yet see,
He's due here today, but didn't show up as planned.

One person standing there in line stepped up to say,
The wind in my ears whispers that he's on his way,
Though in my mind's eye I haven't seen him appear,
My heart of hearts tells me he'll be here for his big day.

Another speaks up, "That's my neighbor, he's so much fun,
Such a caring soul who would help anyone,
The one who would give you the shirt off his back,
Who'd surely win your heart before the day was done."

Very loved and respected, sought out for advice,
Which he doled out freely, no need to ask twice,
Happily telling what to do, how things should be,
Ending it all with that smile, so pleasant and nice.

He liked to talk and talk, and laugh to put you at ease,
He did this all day, everyday, eager to please,
All around the neighborhood his toil kept things neat,
Always a hard worker, mowing lawns and trimming trees.

Hearing all of the good things about his still absent guest,
St Peter nodded in agreement, remembering that Bob's best
And most obvious trademark was his winning smile,
His faithfulness was unshakable when put to the test.

St Peter heard a commotion and turned around,
He knew that his awaited guest had been found,
The newcomer arrived dressed in traditional garb of white,
The one worn by all good folks who are Heaven bound.

Are you Robert, Bobby, or Bob--what's your name?
Yes, that's me, I am he—we are one and the same,
Come on in Bob, we've been waiting for you,
Thank you. I'm late, and I'll take the blame.

I would have been here sooner, so sorry for the delay,
Coming up here I met someone who had lost his way,
He had missed his appointment both the day and the hour,
I just couldn't leave him, he needed me. What could I say?

He couldn't get here alone, he's disabled you see,
Helpless with no one else, he depended solely on me,
So I took him by the hand to guide him to your place,
And we finally arrived here, late though it might be.

Standing behind St Peter was a large crowd of friends,
And kinfolks waiting to greet Bob, to welcome him in,
Anxious to hug him, shake hands, and sing jubilant songs,
Giving high fives, chest and fist bumps to no end.

Approaching the welcome brigade, a wide smile on his face,
Bob stopped, turned and walked back to those Pearly Gates,
I must let everyone know that I'm in good hands,
He looked down to earth thinking, "It's never too late."

Cupping his hands over his mouth, he whispered most sincere,
"I'm OK, I'm good, I made it, I'm finally up here,"
Those joyous words echoed, carried by the wind,
On breezy days they still bring us cheer.

With warmth and much love his words rang out clear,
To my loved ones and family, I am safe at home here,
I'll be waiting for you, though we don't know when,
One day you'll all join me, and I'll see you then.

A Gift Basket of Love for You

I made a gift basket especially for you,
That I prepared and filled with loving care,
To thank you for always being there for me,
For giving me wonderful moments to share.

I thank you for your first warm welcome,
And for quickly taking me under your wing,
For giving me advice, kindness and protection,
For kind words that only a good heart could bring.

Neither years nor distance could keep us apart,
For you're never far from away from my thoughts,
You're part of the rhythm in every beat of my heart,
So I placed hugs and kisses in the basket I brought.

And I humbly offer my prayer, dear sister,
That I tenderly wrapped with my love,
May this little gift help you to feel better soon,
I pray that it will be blessed from above.

Perhaps you feel my presence there with you because,
In mind and spirit I'm with you and always will be,
Quietly standing beside you, so very near,
And I've invited Him to come along with me.

To bring you faith, hope and charity,
And joy in everything you see and do,
As you grow in strength and beauty,
Here is what I wish for you:

That when you open your eyes every morning,
Warm sunlight will greet you after the night hours,
Like silvery drops of dew on fresh new blades of grass,
Or the sweet scented fragrance of wildflowers.

Like whiffs of perfume gently pushed by a balmy breeze,
Or the glorious fuchsia sky during the setting sun,
Like melodious songs of birds high in the trees,
A signal to God's creatures that their day is done.

Like a midnight sky in the golden light of the rising moon,
With serenity and peace He extends His comfort and calm,
Or the bright star that guides you through pleasant dreams,
To the cooling waters sprinkled with Gilead's healing balm.

I've also placed my most heartfelt, precious treasure,
So much more than any material gift can offer,
It is my wish that His touch brings you good health,
This is my solemn prayer to the Great Redeemer.

That He'll take your hand to walk with Him,
And share with you the blessings of His grace,
That He'll guide you to the hem of His garment,
Then He'll wrap you in His warm embrace.

May you always feel His Holy presence,
As He spreads his protective shield over you,
May He renew your spirit and restore your soul,
And inspire you in everything that you do.

Please accept my basket with God's blessings,
That I've made for you with so much love,
My thoughts and prayers are ever with you,
That He'll always smile down on you from above.

And so with steadfast faith I say dear sister,
Just as God has blessed us all with you,
May you be blessed by His healing powers,
And know that His precious love will see you through.

You Are Grace: To My Friend, Miss Sunshine

Under deep blue skies that cover us for protection,
Dimpled with white clouds floating lightly,
Stirred by invisible breezes of sheer perfection,
A rose bud unfurls its beauty ever so slightly.

As nuanced green hues skim over hills and dales,
Shimmering through a haze of dew as far as the eye can see,
Where the sticky-sweet scent of pristine nature prevails,
In a shattering burst of aqua, a red breasted robin comes to be.

Where deer and small animals over arid plains roam,
Where the melodies of the whippoorwill and nightingale compete,
Sending faint echoes to mountains plunging deep into ocean foam,
And unseen sea creatures create new beginnings beneath the reef.

Where paint brushes smear pastels into rainbows across the sky,
After a deluge of cooling waters has cleansed the air,
Soft colors trickle down fields of wildflowers, never to die,
Like candy sprinkles splashing sweet nectar everywhere.

Grace, in our world of hushed but infinite beauty, you are…
The brave moon holding the dreaded night darkness at bay,
The delightful whip of a comet's tail, the twinkle of a shooting star,
The predawn light that opens our eyes to each fresh new day.

The silvery slither of brightness far beyond purple clouds of a storm,
The faint light of the crescent moon, even as darkness looms,
The dusty rose-colored sky at sunset, reappearing at first dawn,
The perfumed scent of an old magnolia tree that forever blooms.

And Grace,

You're the inspiration to be creative, inventive,
The courage that emboldens us to embrace our destiny,
The warmth emanating from a beating heart's incentive,
Giving us strength to continue our life's journey.

You're the warming rays of sunshine,
The smile reaching out from a happy heart,
The quaint but fleeting passage of time,
You're a masterpiece, a work of art.

Here amidst the untapped beauty of our world,
You've been so carefully and gently placed,
Surely there's good reason, and we love who you are,
Your presence is so meaningful because

You

Are

Grace!

Belief in God

In Your Garden

As I sit in your lovely garden
On a still and blissful morn
An unusual calm embraces my soul
As the night quietly yields to dawn.

The sky is blue, a precious blue
Laced with subtle shades of azure
Clouds brushed gently here and there
Fluffed by breezes warm and pure.

In the distance a protective fortress
Majestic mountains of green and brown
Stained with blue and purple hues
Storm clouds encircling their crowns.

Miles of massive mountain forms
Set in rock much like red clay
Worn by erosive winds from tempest storms
Or was it God who sculpted them that way?

As I sit here quietly in your garden
Immersed in peace and tranquility
A balmy breeze soothes my soul
What a mighty God is He!

I am mesmerized here in your garden
Marvel at the billions of stars in the sky
When twilight escapes into the night
How very insignificant am I.

Meditating here in your garden
Amidst birds, shrubs, flowers and all
Surrounding by His omnipotent presence
I am indeed infinitely small.

I'll always remember your garden
Where peace, joy and serenity
Restore my spirit, prepare my body and soul
To abide forever nearer my God to Thee.

Guardian Angels

I'm lucky you opened your eyes today,
I believe in Guardian Angels and often pray,
That your Guardian Angel whoever he may be
Will watch over you, keep you safe for me.

Life can be difficult at times, we know,
But your Angel is with you wherever you go.
When you lose your way, he'll be your guide,
When you need him, he'll be there by your side.

He'll keep you safe from life's harms,
When afraid, he'll enfold you in his arms,
When lonely, he'll come and stay with you,
When times are rough, he'll see you through.

Because of your angel, there's nothing to fear.
Each of God's children has a Guardian Angel near.
Your special angel is right there with you.
Giving you hope, strength and courage too.

He'll comfort you, He'll dry your tears,
And follow you closely through the years.
Filling your soul with love from within,
If you open your heart and let God in.

Forever a friend, you're never alone,
Even after all others have turned and gone.
Although you can't see him, he's always there,
Watching, protecting you with loving care.

Trust in God and you can find happiness.
His goodness and mercy are limitless.
Believe in Him and you'll know it's true,
That through Angels, God takes care of you.

I Believe

I believe that if we help our brother
And follow God's will and way
If we show compassion to one another
God will bless us every day.
I believe that if we are patient
And wait upon the Lord
If we honor, praise and obey Him,
He'll protect us with His mighty sword.

I believe that if we seek His presence
And strive to give Him our all,
He'll carry us over life's highways
Lifting us up each time we fall.
I believe that the things we wish for
No matter how great they are,
Can't compare with God's creations
Not even the tiniest star,

Nor the brooks, lakes and rivers,
Or the mountains built by His hand
Not one of our earthly treasures
Equals the smallest grain of sand.
I believe if we blindly trust Him
Never questioning how or why,
We can calm the raging seas
Pluck twinkling stars from the sky.

I believe that in spirit we're all kings
Possessing wealth and riches untold
And God will fill our hearts and minds
With a knowledge worth more than gold.
I believe that in the simplest things
We can find joy and happiness
With eyes of love we can find the Lord,
In a honey comb, or a tiny sparrow's nest.

The forests, streams and gardens,
And the pine trees standing tall,
The moon that lights our darkened path,
God put them here for us all.
I believe that everything we find on earth,
In the heavens and the oceans too
Are ours if we love Him with all our heart
And believe me, I really do.

God Loves You and So Do We

Last night as I lay on my pillow,
My thoughts soon turned to you.
And thanking God, I said a prayer
Just like I always do.

And I thanked Him for giving us
Everything we have big or small,
That bring real meaning to our lives,
But I thanked Him for you most of all.

He completely filled my heart with love
That was meant with you to share.
And gave me peace and serenity,
To let me know He's always there.

So many things I want to say
I know not where to start…
Perhaps with a simple "I love you"
That's meant with all my heart.

Then in my dreams you came to me,
I saw you sitting there,
With a look of quiet blissfulness,
The sun shining through your hair.

You looked at me and soft, white clouds
Danced lightly in the sky.
In the distance I heard sweet melodies,
From the songbirds' hushed lullabies,

And as you breathed a gentle breeze
Blew softly through the trees.
Just a wisp of air, a mere whisper
Much like the hum of bees.

And I often sit and wonder
Where all of this beauty comes from
By what power, by whose mighty hands
Such magnificent work is done.

The moon, the stars, the rivers wide,
How did they get that way?
The sand, the sea, the mountains high,
What turns night into day?

Then I see the radiance in your face
And I know how they came to be.
From God Almighty, Creator of all things.
His love is for all eternity.

Sometimes we're truly saddened
When things don't go as we plan.
Then he sends His angel down to earth
And bids us to take his hand.

And though we may believe in miracles,
For which in earnest we pray,
'Tis not our will but His will be done.
For our destiny was planned that way.

It is not for us to judge Him,
Nor question the reason why.
But rather to have faith and trust Him.
All things He'll reveal by and by.

Mere mortals are we, and He put us here,
Each with a mission to do.
He knows how well your task is done,
For He dwells within each of you.

When we grow tired and weary,
When there's too much suffering and pain,
He lifts us up on angels' wings,
And calls us home again.

When morning came and I awoke,
I lay in great awe and fear.
For in the silence I felt Him there.
His Holy Presence near.

My aching heart in anguish cried,
Dear Lord, is there anything we can do
To give hope and comfort to those we love?
He replied, "Tell them I love them, and so do you."

Do not despair, for I'll watch over them
And prepare a place with me here.
Where only peace and love abide,
With my loving angels near.

He raised His arms and through the clouds
That suddenly appeared on high,
Your Guardian Angel whispered low,
"God loves you, and So Do I."

So I thank my Master once again,
For sending you this way,
To share your love and life with us.
We're more blessed every day.

Love and Romance

Now That You Are Here with Me: A Wedding Wish

I

Sure, they proudly bragged that their lives were going well,
They spent time doing good deeds, working hard to excel,
They both knew what they wanted, close friends and family,
Let's stop a moment to hear Michelle and Greg's love story.

They'll admit that their jobs were great, as well as things go,
Steadfastly climbing up their career paths, albeit slow.
Taking care not to look back, moving forward to advance,
In their daily lives they were driven; they left nothing to chance.

Content, they lived in their own little worlds, separate and alone,
Singing songs in their heads, each one in a different tone,
Things were looking up, they'd made it; this wasn't bad at all,
Nothing would change, life was good and they were having a ball!

Using good sense, they put irons in the fire, had fingers in every pie,
Things couldn't be better; the ultimate happiness was close by.
Though life alone was routine and dull, and sometimes it was grey,
Our Heavenly Father was sending wonderful changes their way.

Even nature played a fine tune, working wonders in their favor,
It appeared to be producing special feelings they'd soon savor,
The morning sun was warm and the balmy breeze was kind,
Songbirds rehearsed loving melodies time after time.

II

And Then You Came into My Life

Never saw it coming, don't know what happened, can't give it a name,
But since we met, nothing in our lives will ever be the same,
Side by side we dance, gently nudging each other to achieve more,
Making discoveries and seeking adventures behind mysterious doors.

Things that appeared ordinary became spectacular after I met you,
Like bright clouds gingerly floating across skies of the most intense blue.
Birds that chirped and tweeted now play symphonies from trees,
The wind whispers exotic rhapsodies, diffuses fragrant perfume around me.

Wildflowers transform before my eyes into orchids and lotus flowers,
And the time we spend together, how magnificent are those hours.
Streaks of the silvery moon behind purple-blue skies are sure signs
That in the soft, velvety nightfall will forever dawn our love sublime.

And now in our oneness, thoughts and deeds will keep us strong,
We'll stay in each other's arms, for that's where we belong,
Hand in hand we'll walk in God's grace, sharing our love together.
You're a part of my life and I will love and cherish you forever,
Now That You Are Here with Me.

As we witness this Blessed Union, for this we pray,
And we give thanks to our Creator on this lovely day.
For the love Greg and Michelle now share will never end.

May God Bless Them
And Keep Them
Hallelujah Amen.

It Wasn't Meant to Be

Though the hours we spend together are few.
What we feel for each other is a love that's true.
There's a beautiful love between you and me.
That can never bloom because it wasn't meant to be.

I cherish each moment I spend wrapped in your arms.
For when the morning sun rises, I know you'll be gone.
And I'll be left longing for you desperately.
Ours is a love that wasn't meant to be.

Why couldn't we have met at another time.
I'd be yours and you'd be only mine.
Is it luck or fate, or perhaps it's destiny.
By any name, I know it wasn't meant to be.

I lay awake wishing you were here by my side.
Hoping my feelings will become easier to hide.
So I toss and turn like a ship in a stormy sea.
Regretting that our love just wasn't meant to be.

I kiss your lips, you hold my hand.
I'm the Other Woman, you're the Other Man.
But I'll stay in the shadows of infinity.
Fighting for a love that wasn't meant to be.

Sometimes fantasy is better than reality.
That's why I never want you to set me free.
So I'll go on loving you from here to eternity.
Trapped in a love that wasn't meant to be.

For Love of You

You're the first true love I've ever had.
And though you'll never really be mine,
For the love we share I'm truly glad
For love of you.

You're in my mind when times get rough.
You're in my heart when the going gets tough.
The thought of you is more than enough
To keep me loving you.

When we're together, I give you my all.
My body responds love's passionate call.
There's no way I could help but fall
In love with you.

You make me feel like no one can.
You're everything I could ever want in a man.
When you kiss my lips and hold my hand
I know I love you.

I surrender to you in total faith and trust.
My body trembles at your slightest touch.
Only you will ever know how much
I'll always love you.

My Destiny

It was meant to be, it is my destiny
That you should carry me to the highest mountain,
Plunge me to the depths of the deepest sea,
Where love will last an eternity. It was meant to be.

You make my heart soar higher,
My body cries out with desire,
Deeper, deeper into the very heart of me.
It is my destiny, it was meant to be.

When I'm in your arms my mind begins to whirl,
And we spin together into another world.
You're my life, you're everything to me.
This was meant to be, it's my destiny.

You're the one I have always waited for,
You thrill me as no one has ever done before,
Your love is at the heart of every part of me.
It was meant to be, this is my destiny.

You take me to heights of joy unknown,
Into the fires of burning passion I am thrown,
I'll keep loving you until infinity.
It was meant to be, you are my destiny.

The Hawk and the Dove: A Love Story

There's a story I want to tell you
About a hawk and a turtle dove
It carries an inspiring message
About the miracle of love.
One day a proud young hawk was flying
In spiraling circles wide and free
Beating the air with powerful wings.
Then gliding along leisurely.

Without a care in the world, he sailed
With an impressive span of wings.
So engrossed was he in his majesty
That he failed to hear… Pow, Bang, Zing.
Or see the rifle in the enemy's hand
Pointing defiantly towards the sky
And spitting venom… Pow, Bang. Zing.
The hawk was doomed to die.

Stopping the prey in mid-flight
The predator hit its mark
In narrowing circles the young hawk spun
Nose-dived and plunged through the dark.
'Twas meant to be our hero's end
His freedom brutally snatched away,
But this is a loving, heartwarming tale
So it cannot end that way.

Nearby a tiny white turtle dove
Watched in horror and witnessed it all
Saw the young bird proudly soaring
Then suddenly falter, stumble and fall.
Having lost her own beloved mate
And watching him die in pain,
She flew to the where the young hawk lay,
Agonizing under a drizzling rain.

She approached him very carefully,
Placed her body upon his wound
To protect him from the rain and cold
Then later went in search of food.
She stayed with him both day and night
Tending him with loving care
Comforting him in his fight for life
He needed her and she was there.

Then at last he opened his eyes
And heard a soft cooing sound
Remembering the tragic Pow, Bang, Zing.
He looked cautiously all around.
He saw the lovely turtle dove
Hovering close to keep him warm.
Gently fluffing his injured wing,
And protecting him from any harm.

Who is this little creature?
What is she doing here?
Only then did he remember soaring free
Then his impending death was near.
Suddenly something stirred in him
That made his young heart swell
A feeling of love and tenderness
That young hearts know so well.

She looked at him sadly and sighed
A look of longing in her eyes
Now that he was well and strong again
He would fly freely towards the sky.
She had nurtured, tended and healed him
Like a mother cares for her young
So he could now get on with his life
His time with her would be done.

Her head bowed low, she turned to go
But as she prepared to fly away
He gently moved close to her
With his eyes, he begged her to stay.
For a moment, all time stood still
Then she looked to heaven above
And softly said a prayer of thanks
For sending her someone to love.

And so ends this little tale
Of a hawk and a turtle dove
Who will fly together soaring high and free
United in peace and love.

Guest Poets—
All in the Family

There are several poets in my family I want to introduce to you. My Grandmother Helen wrote the following poem that was published in a New Jersey Newspaper when she was 88 years old. My family poets include nieces, nephews, and lots of cousins, some who are still in grade school.

The last poem, ***BONES***, (after the discovery of old African burial sites in Georgetown in Washington, D.C. in September 2012) was written by Melanie Henderson, an accomplished poet. It was first published by Iris G. Press in Fledgling Rag in 2013.

Grandmother Helen Henderson

To Show We Care

Love is something not to be kept but to share
We give it freely to our sister or brother
We lavish it upon father or mother.

The Caregivers love us and help us each day
They share their love and talent in a special way
Through them we are conscious of God's love.

He sends us rain or sunshine straight from above
A kiss or handshake for those folks so dear
Who think of our welfare each day of the year.

To Mom, with Love

You are radiant like the sun
And as bright as the stars.
Your smile is luminous like the moon.
You're the center of my universe
And I love you.

To My Dear Mom

I want to thank you for being you,
The wonderful mom that you are.
You make my days brighter,
You are my shining star.
You are the ray of sunshine on a cloudy day.
You are great in so many ways.
You are precious and priceless
And simply the best.
You are awesome.
Happy birthday mom.

Justin Hemphill, 11

The Rolly Poly (Rolly Poly is a bug)

Rolly Poly rolls in a ball.

Rolly Poly never falls.

Don't get upset. Do not beg.

Rolly Poly lays 200 eggs.

My Shoe

See my shoe.

I have two

They are blue

And they're new.

Justin Hemphill, 12

Justin's Soccer Goal,

The goal was near.

We knew it was mine.

I came from the rear.

To kick past that line.

Jasmine Hemphill, 8

A Day at the Beach

With the sand on my feet
And the breeze in my hair,
I can go to the beach anywhere.

With the sand in my toes
And the sunburn on my nose
I get some ice-cream cones,
It freezes my bones,
At the beach I can't be beat!

If You Were Only One Inch Tall

If you were only one inch tall,
You'd be shorter than a ball.
If you were only one inch tall,
You'd get stuck in gum and fall.
If you were only one inch tall,
Your mother would never call.
If you were only one inch tall,
Your mother would take you to the mall.

Noah Spruill, 10

Sky Diving

Up in the morning,
Into jumpsuit,
Through the door,
In the car,
Up the hill,
On the highway,
Towards the airport,
Inside the plane.
With your friends,
In diving gear,
Off the plane,
In the air,
Against the wind,
About to pull the string,
Beneath the parachute,
With the clouds,
Among the birds,
Towards the ground.
At the end, we land safely.   That is how you sky dive.

Nina Spruill, 12

Memories of Grand Mom

Grand Mom was beauty, love and life.
She had to go, but she's still part of us.
Like the butterfly, she's in another stage.
She toiled first as a caterpillar,
Went dormant before changing
Into a beautiful butterfly.
Grand Mom worked hard.
Temporarily, she had to rest.
With angel wings, she has flown away
To wait for us and be with God.
I love you, Grand Mom

Serena Cross, 10

Serena's Song

I love the sky, it's so blue.
If I had a dog, I would name it that too.
I ride my bike all day long,
And hear the birds sing their song.
I love the way the flowers look,
I would draw them in a book.
Poems are fun and easy too,
Just find that thing inside of you.
I love the way the birds chirp,
It's funny how the froggies burp.
You know that light inside of you?
That bright and bursting thing?
Well you can make it lighter
Just take a breath and sing!!!!

Ernesto Henderson, 14

Life Is Freedom

Life is all about learning
If you learn,
You could earn the right to be free.

Life is a learning experience that earns you power.
When you have power you can reach the top of that tower.

Life is you and me
Can't you see?
It's our destiny
But only if we are free.

Life is more than desire
Unless you want to retire
But wait! Can't you see?
Life is more than that,
It's you, me and everybody!
So don't flee!
Strive to be free!

Life is there for you,
Life is full of glee
So do what's best for you
Life is for us to be free…

Vilma Dianne Bowie-Peele

Impressions of a Forbidden Love

I thought that I could look, and not see
I thought that I could touch, and not feel
I thought that I could want, and not desire
Foolish thoughts of puerility
Had I forgotten that I am woman?
For seeing, feeling and desiring are
        nurtured by the presence
        of that which is sensually
        forbidden—yet, appealing
That I should fall victim to that which
        is desired and desirable—
        though iniquitous to my being
        is inherent to my existence
It is the atavism of my existence
Yet, my altruistic awareness of my depravity
        causes me to crouch absconded in
        the shadow of my shame
Nevertheless, because I am woman
For a moment, out from the darkness
I remember—that I once
Saw, felt, desired
And, yes—loved

Marilyn Bowie-Coates (To My Beloved Sister, Vilma Dianne)

If You Should Leave

If you should leave before me,
surely I will cry, but never hopeless, never asking why.
For this I know, you're in our Father's house.
Your beauty now complete.
And on your face no more pain, no more sorrow
only love, peace and joy remain.
So I'll not say "goodbye" but only "see you soon."
For one day, we will meet again and we will laugh and cry.
But this time there'll be tears of joy so very, very sweet.
For God has said and I believe it's true
that nothing in this world or the world to come
can separate us from the love we share,
for in Christ there is eternity.

Love, Marilyn

BONES by Melanie Henderson

Bonework

Bobcat, crash into my skull,
crack open earth and eat
out the crime, dig in with fat
metal teeth, scoop out land

dismemberment, history
covered over with gardens,
new bricks, sky blue paint,
black about the pains,

call the police, the examiner,
confirm no foul play, archaeologists,
dig me out bone by bone,
mandible, some ribs, joints.

Hurry them here, there is work
to be done, the construction team
is here with hands on their hips,
strong hats about their heads.

Hurry, hurry, remove the skeletons,
the boom crack of ghosts,
rive open the dirt and our bones,
take what you will.

Orchestra

Lay me at the fall line—

I will be more everlasting
than boat, vessel or memory.

You will know my music
when you go to forget me,

my buried bone will rumble
baritone at the shovel's kick,

my band, the river's flow
against uphill rock.

Nostalgia

It's not any different
than Southwest Washington,
or any other old black hood.

Georgetown is marble and
brick over blood and bone.
The tragedy is not its newness

—or even its color. It's a failure
of courtesy not to speak to us:
ghosts on lampposts, right brown

shoes sturdy on left knees,
elbows propping up hatted heads
from the chin; it's a failure

to remember we built those old
rock churches, and monuments,
those houses crumbled to erect

condos that block out light.
Take off your hat when entering
this city; there are spirits around you.

Excavating Spirits

Five wooden coffins with African jaws
inside do not make a sound. An article
in the Post, a brief hault—

our numbers too weak to matter,
our tenure trivial to the home
improvement at shovel.

We'll not bother our cousins, won't dare
rouse the bodies of the Manhattan 400
to voyage South, teach you to let us be,

let our bones lay, prayed over
and untouched. Do not examine
our features for cataloguing,

nor to determine how best we
be used in service of a city
that would rather forget us.

Potpourri

Nature's Palette

Velvety veil of darkness, soft and sweet.
Silhouetted mountain, aquamarine lake at its feet,
Garbed in a robe of glistening white snow,
Nurturing source to crystal waterfalls below.
Jaded forest piercing an opaque silk mist.
Pine-scented breath of the morning's first kiss.
Somber shadows pursued by a bejeweled halo,
Blushes of topaz, amethyst and indigo.
As a golden glow warms from the rising sun,
Sparkling pearl dewdrops embrace the new day begun.
Harvest of beauty laboriously sown.
Magnificent masterpiece by one artist alone.
Silvery flurries of fresh falling snow,
Embellishing our universe created long, long ago.
Marvelous, fascinating planet earth.
Infinite life cycle, glorious rebirth.
Splashes of azure in ice-blue heavens above.
Eternal portrait of
Peace…
Serenity…
and
Love.

Why?

"Why?" her heart cried as tears filled her eyes,
What had gone wrong that her one son should die?
There before her in a quiet, stillness lay
Her hopes for the future, a better life someday.

Alone, despite hundreds of mourners around,
Wrapped in her anguish, no comfort could be found.
Why, her heart screamed in an explosion of rage,
Was he cruelly cut down by boys his own age?

He was so different from the boys in the hood.
He worked hard in school and his grades were quite good.
Role model to the young, a help to the old,
He gave his mom money from the newspapers he sold.

He was a rare treasure, a gem, a source of great pride.
But that night they shot him and all alone he died.
Returning from the library one night around ten,
At the hands of three hoodlums, his young life would end.

Those boys were just looking for trouble, you see.
They were roaming the streets on a murderous spree.
Armed to the teeth, each one had a gun!
As they watched her son die, they thought it was fun.

As she kissed a red rose and tossed it down,
Her loved one slowly disappeared in the ground.
Ashes to ashes, dust to dust.
There must be a reason why… dear God,
There must!

There, but for the Grace of God Go You (The Beggar)

I

He sat silent on the corner
A paper cup in his hand,
Looking up, his face said, "Please,"
But his eyes said, "I am a man."
I stopped and stared and as I did,
His bent form straightened tall.
Those deep sad eyes reflected hurt,
Desperation, despair,... no hope at all.
In another place or some other time,
I might have passed him by.
More than his clean clothes and shave,
It was his anger caught my eye.
I quickened my step and looked away
As I have so often done,
Beggars rarely touch my heart,
Why should I help this one!
After a few minutes had gone by,
I heard murmurs from Satan clearly say,
"Those disgusting beggars are everywhere!"
And then indignant, I walked away.
I'm sick and tired of seeing them
They're lazy, slick and rude.

II

While they're holding out their hands to us,
We're working hard to buy food.
Why should we feel more than contempt?
They don't deserve our pity.
They have no shame, no sense of worth,
No pride, no dignity.
Like the one I saw two weeks ago
Who, when I shook my head,
Hurled angry insults at my back.
I was shocked by what he said.
And the ones who continue to cheat us all,
Begging coins from passers by,
Then depositing their "profits" in the bank.
Tax free, they're worth more than you and I.
Not long ago I gave some change
To a beggar on the street,
Claiming to be just down on his luck,
Saying he needed a bite to eat.
But I saw him again at 5 o'clock
Staggering out of a package store,
With a bottle of cheap wine and a great big grin!
With that I said, "No more!"

III

That convinced me I was justified
Not to let any of my money go,
To change their kind into lazy bums
So, I've learned to just say, "No."
The other day a strong young man
Lay prostrate on the street.
Unlit cigarette in his hand,
No shoes upon his feet.
And while he lay there on his back
Being baked by the morning sun,
His young life was slipping past.
Time will wait for no one.
My conscience began to bother me,
And urged me to lend a hand,
Who am I to judge his need,
Or the plight of my fellow-man?
So I went on back and dropped a bill
In the cup he held in his hand.
Through lips drawn tight, he murmured, "Thanks."
While his eyes said, "I'm still a man."

IV

And now I think I understand
His resentment to indifference and neglect.
Whether hungry, homeless or unemployed,
Every man deserves our respect.
About six months later a man approached,
Dressed in suit, white shirt and tie.
He seemed to be intently studying me
With a curious look in his eye.
He hesitated, then he softly asked,
"Do you remember me?"
Dumbfounded, I said "Is that you,
The beggar…? No, it can't be!"
He broke into a hearty laugh,
Then gently took my hand,
And placed in it a dollar bill,
He was truly a different man.
His eyes, now bright with faith and hope
Were no longer filled with pain,
And looking deep down within I knew
That he'd found his pride again.

V

"I'm not the man you saw that day.
Sometimes it's hard, you see.
I have a wife and three young kids
And they all depend on me.
How can a man who has lost his job
Come home with empty hands?
But being unemployed, destitute and poor,
Doesn't make him any less of a man.
For I had to beg out on the street
To buy food, clothes and pay rent.
When I lost my job six months ago,
We were left without a cent.
So what you thought you saw that day
Wasn't bitterness at all,
But rather the care I had to give
To make sure that I would recall,
Each and every generous soul
Who helped me on the street,
So I could pay them back in full
When I got back on my feet."

VI

So the moral of this little poem
And there is one, you know…
"Show love and compassion all the time,"
For one day, you'll reap what you sow.
Follow your heart in every deed!
Never feel you are a fool.
Do unto others… you know rest,
It's called the "Golden Rule."
You may have a house, a car and cash
And feel you're doing well.
But who knows what tomorrow will bring?
Only God knows, only time will tell.
Don't turn your back on your fellow man.
Show compassion in all you do.
Help those who are less fortunate, and never forget, that
There, but for the Grace of God Go You!

Cry for Africa - The Lost Continent

A nameless face,
A baby's feeble cry.
In this harsh world,
Innocent masses die.
Cruel dictators raise their hands,
Spreading death and destruction over barren lands.
DISEASE!
FAMINE!
MASSACRES!
No death more atrocious than one of these.
Men, women, children drop like flies.
It's an internal thing, this genocide,
So the world looks on indifferently nearby,
While God's children die… the people die, and they die!
By hundreds of thousands and we don't even try,
To help them survive, until it's too late.
Much too late!
No, genocide is nothing new,
Ethiopia, Uganda, Sudan, Darfur, Rwanda
And Mali too.
We pretend we don't know what to do.
Why?
The question is no longer Why,
But HOW?
How can we look into pleading, listless eyes,
See millions of emaciated bodies along the wayside,
And not react NOW?
History often repeats itself.
We've seen this all before.
We possess power and wealth.
We can and we must do more.
The lessons of human compassion are there to learn
Will you answer the call when it's your turn?

A Tribute to My Best Friend Helen

We're happy and sad to be celebrating this day.
Can't escape or ignore it, won't go away.
We saw it was coming, but didn't want to know,
The Countdown slipped from DAY 3, 2, 1, then BINGO!
I closed my eyes and covered my ears,
But the flyers and memos confirmed my worse fears!
So you're really doing it, you're retiring at last,
They'll have to pry us apart, the bond is stuck fast.
You know, 'round the office, when they saw you, they saw me,
If I was alone, it was, "Hey, where's your buddy?"
Reality finally hit me, the inevitable moment has come true,
Now I'm wondering, "What in the world I'll do without you!"
How I'll survive remains to be seen,
My rose-colored glasses have turned envious green.
I'll miss you each morning, when you called just to say,
"Hi girl, I'm here. How are you today?"
From our lunch-time walks just to "clear the air,"
Filled with mischievous gossip, girl, "Don't even go there!"
To our foolproof scheme of Balances and Checks.
I'd drag you from Nordstrom's, you'd ban me from Hecht's!
At times there were glitches and our "system" fell through,
Girl get out your gold card, that dress is YOU!
At the office or at home, we'd soon find a way,
To be close to each other, or not far away.
At a crab feast, seminar or Sweetheart's Ball,
Taking "sick" leave together, then heading straight to the mall.
Discretion could well be your middle name,
Can't speak for you, but my life won't be the same!
You worked with confidence, pride and dignity,

In a highly professional manner, a master of diplomacy.
Your smile and pleasant manner are by nature, not design,
With strength, wisdom and quick humor, you're one of a kind.
Never heard you refuse, reject or decline,
Never heard you say, "Get your own, I've already got mine."
You "duked it out" with the young staff, made war at the top,
Had your last nerve plucked raw 'till your composure was shot.
You've been through the mill and the wringer, served time in salt mines,
After 35 years of hard labor, you're cruising to PRIME time!
You say now you're ready to leave the workforce,
Our nods of approval show you've made the right choice.
You can lay back, do aerobics, travel long, far and wide,
Go prancing and line dancing, do the "Electric Slide!"
Don't stop now, we've been partying together since 1992,
But to enjoy life to the fullest, it really takes two!
You can sleep late, learn quilting like some retirees do,
Yeah, I'll be dragging to work, but I'll be thinking about you!
I wish you happiness, prosperity and especially good health,
But I'll be eating without you, alone, all by myself!
Wait just a minute, not too fast, there's too much at stake,
No more of your homemade sweet potato pie or red velvet cake!
Good luck, my dear friend. I'm wishing you well in all you do,
Keep us in mind because we'll sorely miss you,
As I wind down and end this farewell tribute,
We raise our glasses to you in a rousing salute!

A Tribute *to Lady Joan, First Lady of St Mary's Baptist Church*

Who knows Lady Joan?
This strong, prayerful woman that we've all come to know,
Faithful to her childhood sweetheart, whom she married 46 years ago,
Mother of two sons, grandmother of two granddaughters, and it's easy to see,
That each one of them will proudly ensure her life's legacy.

Who knows Lady Joan?
We've witnessed her presence ever stunning and new,
Especially when wearing her favorite color of blue,
Her knowledge of what's trendy is in vogue and in style,
But the spark of high fashion dims in the light of her winning smile.

Who knows Lady Joan?
Humility and patience have kept her forever strong,
For this dedicated teacher, education is her life song,
As the New Members of the Church are keenly aware,
When in need of guidance she's always been there.

Who knows Lady Joan?
Her devotion to the church is well known indeed,
Going out of her way to help our brothers in need,
Her dedication to our missionary ministry extends far and near,
She is very special, our Lady Joan, whom we hold very dear.

Who knows Lady Joan?
Her kindness expands outward, we feel it to no end,
Not surprisingly, she wanted to write books for children,
To teach life's good lessons to those fresh little minds,
We hope she'll fulfill that dream, now there'll be more time,

Who knows Lady Joan?
Well we all know her, with her big heart and keen mind,
She has always had a passion for writing a birthday rhymes,
And on those special birthdays each and every year,
Her melodies are heard across phone lines, her voice crystal clear.

Who has met Lady Joan?
Everyone who's met her can assure you there's so much more,
And our missionary ministry has a lot to be truly grateful for,
There's one thing she has in common with many of you,
I need only to mention that she's native Washingtonian too.

We are pleased and proud to present Lady Joan,
To be counted among friends, you must certainly have guessed,
That to know her and love her, our missionaries are very blessed.
And we are here to give notice that for this reason alone,
Today it is our great privilege to honor our ***First Lady Joan.***

I'm Not There Yet! (My Retirement)

Don't ask me if I'm there yet,
Ask rather where I'm going,
The answer is not for today because
That depends how destiny's wind is blowing.

Don't ask me how I'll get there,
Watch my steps and the direction I tread,
Every day brings a new challenge,
To be woven in my life's tapestry thread.

Don't worry if I'll make it there,
Change means that what used to be is no more,
The question should instead be "When?"
Facing obstacles, life will open another door.

Don't wonder when I'll reach my goals,
You may think I can't, but don't laugh,
One day I'll fulfill all of my dreams,
Though more are waiting to cross my path.

Don't doubt for a minute that I can make it,
For this very moment will become, "back then."
And tomorrow, today will be yesterday,
Renewing opportunities again and again.

Time is irrelevant at this point in my life,
Into my future I'm compelled to reach,
For the guarantee that I'll never stop learning,
From all things my life has to teach.

So I'll keep moving forward inch by inch,
And as my intrepid footprints lead away,
No matter what pathway they may take,
They'll surely get me to the top someday.

No, don't ask me if I'm there yet,
Come with me, close your eyes, dare to dream,
We can illuminate the places we're going,
Only if we make a difference in the places we've been.

We've Been Waiting for You

(Inauguration of Barack Obama 2008)

Fruit of generations of hopes and prayers,
Pride swelling our hearts like a thousand drumbeats,
Emerging from clouds surrounding the highest mountaintop,
Illuminating shadows, leaving a valley bathed in sun.
Worthy heir of that long-ago dream,
Aurora of sunshine, overflowing with inner peace,
We've been waiting for you.

Humbly you've come to lead our nation in healing,
A nation devoured by destructive elements from within,
Torn by strife, its lifeline devastated by greed,
Weakened by wars on distant shores, troubled waters flowing deep,
You come forth, a bright force shining through the darkness,
A ray of sunshine beaming through skies of blue.

You stand before us with a promise, with outstretched hand,
Pulling us from the edge of the abyss by sheer strength of character,
Intelligent, endowed with foresight and wisdom beyond your years,
Desiring peace for all humanity, offering your soothing, fragrant balm,
Overcoming hard times from your own humble beginnings,
That a loving family and faith helped you get through.

Loved by many, putting smiles on our faces, warmth in our hearts,
Transcending all barriers, admired even by your opponents,
Inspiring powerful leaders of nations around the world,
With keen perception you envision unity for us all,
You are one of us, a part of each of us,
Making us believe we can make a difference too.

A spirit of oneness is your message to everyone,
People from all walks of life helping one another,
Renewing confidence, invigorating us to move forward,
Standing before a country divided and confused,
Encouraging us to again become "One Nation under God,"
We're ready to start anew.

Prime example of freedom, of inalienable rights,
Embodiment of what is needed in these troubled times,
Restoring our belief that we are all created equal,
That we can bring about change. Yes, we can,
The time has come to lead, the time is now,
We put our trust in you.

As you prepare to lead us in this historic moment,
We applaud your sense of urgency, your desire to turn things around,
Bringing with you the lovely First Family for all to share,
Beautiful in every sense of the word,
Step up and take your place in the history of our great Nation,
Barack Obama, Mr. President,
We've been waiting for you!

America, Could We Love You More?

I

America, could we love you more?
Than Maryland's Sugarloaf Mountain presiding over lush valleys below,
Than rows of wheat in the heartlands of Indiana, Iowa and Idaho,
Or ebbing tides in the Pacific Northwest where two great rivers flow,
Than treasures discovered deep below that Virginia's Shenandoah caverns bore.
America, could we love you more?

Than neat rows of corn in Kansas stretching as far as the eye can see,
And the Midwest where herds of buffalo, deer and antelope still roam free,
Than the welcoming wave to immigrants from our Lovely Lady Liberty,
"Enlightening the World" like she did on her *grande entrée* over 126 years before.
America, could we love you more?

Than the Alaskan tundra where Iditarod mushers run the world's last great race,
Or Hawaiian orchids creating fragrant leis around each dormant volcano's face,
Than the Denver sky gently reaching past stars seeking an angel's embrace,
Or California surfers chasing dreams in waves well beyond the ocean's roar.
America, could we love you more?

Than paddle-wheel boats lazily cruising along the mighty River Mississippi,
Or the arid deserts of Chihuahuan and Mojave, the awe-inspiring Death Valley,
Than the American bald eagle's triumphant return to nesting in Tennessee,
Or American Indian flutes paying tribute to ancestral spirits through folklore.
America, could we love you more?

Than clams and lobsters baking over beach bonfires on a New England night,
Or the flutter of wings in a Magnolia tree as game partridges take flight,
Than savoring Georgia peach cobbler and pecan pies with gourmet delight,
And tasting sweet Chesapeake crab cakes from Maryland's Eastern Shore.
America, could we love you more?

II

Than vestiges of covered bridges in Madison County defiantly lingering around,
Or the Everglades of Florida where bullfrogs, snakes and crocodiles abound,
Than Yuma where an entire year of unbelievably sunny days can be found,
Or Baltimore's Inner Harbor where the ghost of Poe's Raven echoes, "Nevermore."
America, could we love you more?

Than the revered fields of Gettysburg, Bunker Hill and Harper's Ferry,
Sacred battlegrounds where perpetual reenactments boast your glorious history,
Where the bravery of beloved heroes is never doubted, nor their courage a mystery,
Reinforcing our profound belief in Freedom, Justice, Equality, and so much more.
America, could we love you more?

Than northern Lake Superior, Huron, Michigan, Ontario and Erie,
Or South Carolina's brilliance from each vividly colored Crepe Myrtle Tree,
Or the elk and moose seen grazing high in the massive Mountain Rockies,
Or where festive beads are tossed at the New Orleans Mardi Gras as never before.
America, could we love you more?

Than the sprays of iridescent mists unveiling eternal rainbows at Niagara Falls,
Or where silent winds carry the Mourning Dove's sweet mating call,
Where from breathtaking heights we experience humility, dignity, splendor and all,
Where butterflies and hummingbirds sprinkle their beauty deep within your core.
America, could we love you more?

Than wisps of white cotton portraying exotic caresses in clear blue skies,
Or rain-soaked prairies glistening from the morning dew at sunrise,
Where nocturnal creatures usher in the dawn, sleepily closing their eyes,
In stark contrast to our forefathers' eternal vigilance on Mount Rushmore.
America, could we love you more?

III

My beautiful country, please hear my humble plea,
Let us return to the great nation that we were meant to be,
Loving you unconditionally as we have throughout your proud history!
So again, I pause to beg the question, America, could we love you more?

When we are outwardly tolerant of the differences between each other,
When we believe a man of every race, religion, and creed is our brother,
When we continue to open our borders, welcoming those in need,
And extend our hands to the oppressed and disenfranchised seeking liberty.

When we learn to use the mighty pen instead of a gun, knife or sword,
To defend our inalienable rights and to pursue happiness as ultimate rewards,
When we kindle love in our hearts to keep the melting pot forever warm,
When hatred and evil deeds become the exception, never the norm.

When the freedom bought by deploying to foreign lands our daughters and sons,
Is more valuable to us than the place where a person's life was begun,
When we spread our love and share our wealth over this bountiful land,
And within our hearts we wish peace on earth, good will to our fellow man.

When One Nation under God, Indivisible is where we will stand proud and tall,
America the Beautiful, My Country 'tis of thee, with liberty and justice for all,
When we've finally chased racism, bigotry and hatred far away from our shores,
Then America, we can and we will surely love you even more!
America Strong Forever!

My Legacy in Poetry and Prose

That's What Grandmas Do!

So much time I want to spend with you,
So many exciting things we can do,
It's so easy to spoil you, give you nice things, it's true,
Because as we all know, that's what Grandmas do.

Perhaps we'll travel the world together, cross a few continents,
Climb mountains, hike nature trails, even pitch our tents,
Sail the seas, swim the oceans, discover caves in time well spent,
See the wonders of our planet, explore the world to our heart's content.

Holding you deep in my heart because of the joy you've brought,
Carefully guiding you, keeping each of you deep in my thoughts,
As we walk along hand in hand, I'll keep you near,
Protect you from harm because Grandma holds you dear.

Staying one step behind you, ready to catch you if you fall,
Throughout life's journeys, I'll be there to answer your call,
Moving obstacles from your pathway as we leisurely walk,
Giving hope and confidence, you know, "Grandma" talk.

I'll keep you safe, give you love and comfort in every way I can,
Showing you wonderful treasures, going to far away lands,
Leading the way, teaching you, keeping you up to speed,
Helping you to find your way; Grandma knows what you need.

Showering you with affection with your best interest in mind,
Developing your potential, fulfilling your dreams over time,
I'm right behind you with the support you know so well,
Waiting in the wings like Grandma Guardian Angel.

I'll be there when you pass through every important milestone,
Marveling at your life's stages, saying, "My how you've grown!"
Graduating from college, getting your first job, walking down the isle,
You may not see me, but you can feel my presence, imagine my smile.

And even when I'm no longer with you, I'll be near, never too far,
Perhaps I'll be watching you from beyond a twinkling star,
Lighting the way, watching over you, forever your guide,
You can rest assured I'm out there, filled with Grandma's pride.

As you step out into the world, test your wings, give life a try,
Think of the good times you shared with your Grandma nearby,
You may hear my voice in the wind, feel my warmth in the air,
Or visualize me in cloud formations, I'll be somewhere out there.

Yes, dear children, I'll be there beside you, behind you,
Giving advice, whispering words of wisdom too,
Applauding each success as it makes its way to you,
All the while praising you from the shadows, because…
that's what Grandmas do!

A Message to My Precious Grandchildren, Brianna, Grace and Xavier

I realize that there are four generations between us. That's good, because I believe I have some experience that could help each of you fulfill your dreams. I want you to know that I see great things for each one of you in the future. You have a wonderful heritage from the generations that walked the trails before you. Like all good ancestors would do, yours worked in the fields and tended gardens filled with thorns so that you will be able to bloom free, full of strength and beauty. How lucky you are to have your heritage spread out three over continents: 1) the European Continent, specifically in France, with its extraordinary cultural and artistic history and love for Les *Beaux Arts*; 2) the South American Continent, going back to Guatemala where the first cultures of the Mayan Indians were among the most advanced of ancient times; and finally, 3) the North American Continent, despite slavery, hardships and obstacles, your roots bore rich fruit and bouquets of flowers in the Nation's Capital. These are invaluable treasures that not many people will ever know. You have untold jewels in your past. More importantly, there are treasures waiting for you out there today. I'm confident that you will have extraordinary futures as you profit from these advantages. One thing I ask is that you don't grow and bloom *only* in your own back yards. Reach out, travel the world, learn about our planet and explore the universe. Strive to make your mark and leave your legacy!

I am certain that you will continue to use your heritage as stepping stones to do great things. I know this because you are my precious, cherished grandchildren. So, please read my words, my sincere and humble words. I hope you will be able to feel my pride and love for you. Always remember that I love each of you in a special way. Believe me when I say that I am blessed to have the three of you as my grandchildren.

My loving wish for you is to stay well and be happy in all you do.

About the Author

Carrolyn Pichet, a native Washingtonian, began working for the DC Parole Board before graduating from the Spingarn High School Honors Programs. Career positions followed with the Interstate Parole Board, Peace Corps, African-American Institute and the International Military Sports Council. She received a B. A. Degree in Romance Languages from Howard University, with Phi Beta Kappa and Cum Laude honors. After attending the University of Maryland for a Masters Degree in Spanish Language and Literature, she received a grant from the International Institute of Education to teach in French high schools in Avignon and Nice, France. Returning to the US, she worked with the Congressional Banking Committee, then for twenty years with the USNCB, Interpol, Justice Department. She retired from the Language Services Section of the FBI in 2009.

The author's first book, *The Best Is Yet to Come*, a mind and body motivational book, was published in 2011. Her second, *Growing Up in the Nation's Capital: We Made It, But It Took an Entire Village*, was published in May, 2013. An avid lover of the fine arts, she enjoys storytelling and participating in speech and writing contests. She is following her grandmother's footsteps and fulfilling her dreams writing, reciting and interpreting poetry.

www.ingramcontent.com/pod-product-compliance
Ingram Content Group UK Ltd.
Pitfield, Milton Keynes, MK11 3LW, UK
UKHW040601210726
13854UKWH00008B/1664

9 781491 848654